Contents

Foreword

The words which we use during Holy Week and Easter are often so familiar that we do not realise their meaning may need some unpacking for those who listen to them. Denial, sacrifice, repentance, even resurrection itself: what do these abstracts really mean? Stories and poems can often show us – can explain and illuminate, even when the context is one of everyday life and apparently not connected at all with things religious. Perhaps, indeed, especially then.

The extracts and poems in this anthology are, therefore, taken from a number of sources, not all of them predictable and some of them even surprising. Many of them come from children's books – a good children's book often deals with a theme of powerful and universal appeal and, as C. S. Lewis said, may be enjoyed as much by those of fifty as by those of ten. Here, therefore, you will find Fay Sampson and Penelope Lively, E. B. White and Russell Hoban, as well as Lewis himself. These are all pieces which could be used with adults and children together, as well as with groups of children alone.

Perhaps their links with the Easter story of the Bible are not always clear at first glance. They are nevertheless there. Sometimes the words heading the extracts will help: it is easy to parallel 'arrest', for instance, with that other moment, in Gethsemane, when the soldiers came. Sometimes there is an explicit Christ-figure in the extract; Aslan the lion is now well-known, but Arthmael the dolphin is less so – yet read of him 'powering up through all the layers of creation' and then turn to Colossians 1. 13-20... Leon Garfield's Possul, with his torchlight, is full of resonances: the Good Samaritan, Matthew 25. 31-46 and John 1.5 above all. Old Hewitson, in Jane Gardam's *The Hollow Land,* brings to mind the definition of faith in Hebrews 11. 1-3, never translated better than by the Authorised Version: 'Now faith is the substance of things hoped for, the evidence of things not seen'.

Through stories and verse this book tries to bring the words of Easter alive – to help its readers to share and understand more vividly the experiences of Good Friday and Easter Sunday and their consequences for us all ... without end...

Pamela Egan

Words *for* Easter

An Anthology

compiled by Pamela Egan

NATIONAL SOCIETY/CHURCH HOUSE PUBLISHING
Church House, Great Smith Street, London SW1P 3NZ

2

ISBN 0 7151 4791 9

Published 1990 for The National Society jointly by The National Society and Church House Publishing, Church House, Great Smith Street, London SW1P 3NZ

Cover by Bill Bruce

Printed by Orphans Press Ltd., Hereford Road, Leominster, Herefordshire, England.

Hot Cross Buns

(In a little south coast town during the Napoleonic Wars the Oliver family keeps a bakery in Simnel Street. They are preparing for Good Friday.)

Abram was in the bakehouse on Thursday afternoon, mixing the dough for the following day. For once there would be no breakfast rolls, no bread, no cake; nothing but a thousand hot cross buns, each with a bold cross of almond paste on the shiny dark crust. Many families kept a hot cross bun in the kitchen all year round, for luck and blessing; it would dry out and harden, but never turn mouldy. Abram took down last year's from the bakehouse chimney-piece and put the first of this year's baking in its place.

Jenny Overton
(from 'The Ship from Simnel Street')

Hot cross buns! Hot cross buns!
One a penny, two a penny,
Hot cross buns!
If you have no daughters,
Give them to your sons,
One a penny, two a penny,
Hot cross buns!

Traditional

Easter Eggs

(Susan Garland – who is really the author Alison Uttley – lived on a Derbyshire farm with her parents Tom and Margaret in the 1890s. Susan had never seen an Easter egg, for such luxuries were not to be found in the local village shop, until –)

Last Easter Mrs Garland had called at the vicarage with her missionary box and taken Susan with her. Mrs Stone had asked Margaret to make some shirts for the heathen, and whilst they had gone in the sewing-room to look at the pattern, Susan, who had been sitting silent and shy on the edge of her chair, was left alone.

The room chattered to her; she sprang up, wide-awake, and stared round. She had learnt quite a lot about the habits of the family from the table and chairs, when her eye unfortunately spied a fat chocolate egg, a bloated enormous egg, on a desk before the window. Round its stomach was tied a blue ribbon like a sash.

Susan gazed in astonishment. What was it for? She put out a finger and stroked its glossy surface. Then she gave it a tiny press of encouragement, and, oh! her finger went through and left a little hole. The egg must have been soft with the sunshine. But who would have thought it was hollow, a sham?

She ran and sat down again, deliberating whether to say something at once or to wait till she was alone with her mother. Mrs Stone returned with Margaret saying, 'Yes, Mrs Stone, of course I won't forget the gussets. The heathen jump about a good deal, they will need plenty of room.' But before Susan could speak, a long-haired, beaky-nosed girl ran into the room, stared at Susan and went straight to the Easter egg.

'Who's been touching *my* Easter egg?' she cried, just like the three bears.

They all looked at Susan and with deep blushes she whispered, 'I did.'

They all talked at once; Margaret was full of apologies and shame, Mrs Stone said it didn't matter, but of course you could see that it did, and the bear rumbled and growled.

When she got home, Susan had to kneel down at once and say a prayer of forgiveness, although it was the middle of the morning.

Alison Uttley
(from 'The Country Child')

Easter Cakes

(The bakery on Simnel Street prepares for Easter Sunday)

On the morning of Easter Saturday, Abram started work on the solly cakes for the following day. They were fashionable, expensive and troublesome, needing the finest wheat flour, sieved through silk, and new milk warm from the cow. Billy set to work in the bolting-room, sifting the best flour through three tammy sieves, the first with a mesh of sixty, the second ninety, and the third a hundred and twenty holes to the inch. The dairymaid from Saltings Farm brought her best cow through the streets and milked her, then and there, in the yard. Col carried pails of warm foamy milk into the bakehouse, and the cats came streaming after him. 'Turn them creatures out, boy,' Abram said. He shouted up the stairs to Billy, 'Make haste, lad! You'll never set the tams afire at that rate.'

Jonathan liked to make his own yeast, using his father's recipe, (a mixture of hops and potatoes), but to save time and trouble Abram had begun buying ale barm from Nye's Brewery. He sniffed the newest barm, which was brown and pungent; crumbled a scrap in his fingers; and thought it over. 'Reckon not,' he said. 'Fetch up last Wednesday's, Sam. It'll take longer to work, but the flavour's milder – better suited to the best wheat flour.'

The solly-cake dough was left to rise in the bakehouse all day long. The dairymaid brought back the cow that evening, milked her again, and promised to deliver cream on Easter morning. Susannah helped to mix more flour, salt and sugar, and the new milk into a thick paste ready for kneading. She scooped up a handful of the fine wheat flour and let it run through her fingers. It was creamy white, dappled with bran and flecked gold from the wheat kernels. White and golden brown and cream, she thought, as Josh showed her how to fold in the starter dough: Easter colours...

She woke in the blowy dark before dawn. In the bakehouse the keelers were full of solly-cake dough, fragrant and alive. She helped to shape it into small rounds which were set to rise on the baking sheets. Sam was trying to copy Josh who could roll two at a time, one in each hand, expertly. The delivery boys arrived early, ready to sell hot cakes from door to door in time for breakfast.

As soon as the cakes came out of the ovens, light and crisp, pale as ivory, Josh brushed them over with egg-yolk glaze, and it set deep gold in the warmth of the fresh-baked dough. The boys began to wrap them in linen cloths and stow them in the baskets. Solly cakes were a West Country speciality, split open, spread with clotted cream, and eaten hot. Jonathan's emigré friend, Mr Lemarchand, had told him that 'solly' was a French name, *soleil lune*, meaning 'sun and moon', and as Susannah helped to pack them, this Easter morning, she saw why.

'The yellow sun above and the white moon below,' she said to Abram, pleased.

Abram grunted. 'Sounds like a good sturdy English name to me,' he said stubbornly. 'Thought your Da got the recipe from that cousin a' yours down in Bath?'

'So he did, but – oh well,' Susannah said. 'It doesn't matter. I only meant the carol fits the cakes.'

The boys went down Simnel Street with the baskets on their heads, Tom Herring blowing blithely on his pipe:

It was on Easter Day,
And all in the morning,
Our Saviour arose,
Our own heavenly king:
The sun and the moon
They did both rise with him:
And sweet Jesus we call him by name.

Jenny Overton
(from 'The Ship from Simnel Street')

Light and Darkness

(Possul, an orphan boy who is apprenticed to a lamplighter in eighteenth-century London, works after dark as a linkboy; he waits outside a coffee-house with a torch made of burning pitch, to light gentlemen home through the dark streets for payment of a few coppers.)

'Light you home, sir?'

'Take me to Clifford's Inn, child. Do you know it?'

''S off Chancery Lane.' The gentleman nodded and Possul set off. Presently a low noise in a cleft between two houses distracted him. He held out his torch. A woman and a nearly naked child were huddled together in an attempt to get warmth from each other. The woman, half blinded by the sudden light, looked savage at the intrusion on her misery. Possul paused, as if to give his gentleman full benefit of the sight.

'Get a move on, boy,' he said. 'It's no business of ours in there.'

Possul withdrew the torch and left the cleft in decent darkness. A little while after, he stopped again. A legless beggar, who squatted on a porridge pot and got about by dragging himself by fist and fingernail over the cobbles, squinted up from the entrance to an alley. Every detail of his misfortune was pitiless in Possul's leaping fire.

'Get along with you,' said the gentleman. 'Find something better worth looking at.'...

Just outside the gate to Clifford's Inn, a youngish woman was humped against a wall and crying. Possul lingered, and his torchlight shone on her tear-stained face, revealing harsh bruises and dried blood.

'That's enough,' said the gentleman. 'When I want to be shown the miseries of the night, I'll employ you again. Till then, my lad, keep out of my way.'

He gave Possul only threepence and dismissed him...

On the seventh day it rained... The rain was not heavy; it was more of a fine drizzle, a weeping of the night air that made the torch hiss and spit... A man came out of the coffee-house on his own... He was a huge elephant of a fellow, untidily dressed and wearing a frown as if he'd bought it as suiting his particular cast of features. He squinted balefully at Possul's fire.

'Light you home, sir?'

The man grunted ill-temperedly, searching his capacious mind, and came out with: *'Take heed therefore that the light which is in thee be not darkness.'*

He sniffed and wiped his nose against the back of his hand.

'Well?'

'Yes, sir. I'll take heed. Where to, sir?'

'Red Lion Square. D'you know it?'

'Off High Holborn, ain't it?'

'Thereabouts. Lead on.'

Possul lifted up his torch and went; the large man lumbered after. The rain, although not increasing, had soaked the streets, so that the torch, reflecting upon the streaming cobbles, ran along like a river of broken fire... At last they turned into Grays Inn Passage; the torch flickered across a bundle of rags heaped against a doorstep. As if unable to help himself, the link-boy paused. The huge fellow lurched and swayed to a halt.

'What d'you think you're doing, boy?'

'Nothing – nothing, sir. It's just me torch ... shining, shining on...' He jerked the light apologetically towards the doorstep. The bundle of rags leaped out of the night; it contained a twig of a woman with arms and cheeks as thin as leaves. She was either dead or so close to it that it would have taken a watchmaker to tell the difference...

Possul brought his torch closer to the woman's face. Her skin was blotched and covered with open sores that the rain had made to shine... Suddenly a twist of blue flame — no bigger than a finger — danced up above her mouth; then it vanished with extraordinary rapidity. It was as if the spark of life had been made visible, departing.

'Get back,' grunted the man, pushing Possul away with his cudgel. 'She's full of gin. You saw it? That gasp of fire above her lips. The torch set it off. Get away. It's not for you and me to burn her before her time.'

He gave Possul another shove, swore malevolently at the night — and bent down, so that every stitch of his clothing protested at the effort. He picked up the gin-sodden, diseased creature as easily as if she'd been a frayed old coat; then he heaved her on his back.

'Move on,' he said to Possul.

'Where to, sir?'

'My house. Would you have me carry this unwholesome burden farther?'

'What will you do with her, sir?'

'Eat her. Plenty of pepper and salt. Then I'll give her bones to my cat.'

The creature that was flopped across his back emitted a raucous moan.

'Peace, ma'am, peace. Presently you shall have comfort and warmth. Hurry, boy, hurry, before we're all poisoned by the stink of her gin.'

In a moment, Possul's fire broke out into Red Lion Square and cast the large man's shadow with its misshaped double back against the fronts of the stately houses; it seemed impossible for those within not to feel the dark passing...

Presently the fire and shadow halted. Then the shadow grew enormous and engulfed one particular house... Cautiously, and with solemn gentleness, the shadow's owner took off his hump and laid the tattered woman against his front door while he fumbled for a coin to pay the linkboy.

Why was the night suddenly so dark? He stood up and turned. The boy with the torch had vanished. The square was empty and without light. He fancied he glimpsed a flickering coming from the direction of Fisher Street, which was some way off. It might have been the light of a linkboy; then again, it might not. The woman at his feet moaned again; he banged ferociously and urgently on his front door. He looked again towards Fisher Street, but the light had gone. He shook his head as if to rid it of a memory that was already faltering into disbelief. His front door opened, and before he went inside, he stared upwards as if for the sight of a new star. Nothing — nothing but blackness and rain.

Leon Garfield
(From 'The Apprentices')

Light and Darkness

The sun is soon to rise as bright

As if the night had brought no sorrow.

That grief belonged to me alone,

The sun shines on a common morrow.

You must not shut the night inside you,

But endlessly in light the dark immerse.

A tiny lamp has gone out in my tent –

I bless the flame that warms the universe.

Friedrich Rueckert

Take, Eat

(At his Last Supper with his friends, Jesus broke bread and blessed it; he blessed the wine and shared both with his friends. Then he told them, 'Take, eat... Do this in remembrance of me.' From this came the Christian Church's service of Holy Communion.)

Lord, at the Last Supper with your Apostles
You gave them the command
To break bread and bless wine,
Just as you had done.
It was to be your memorial, you said.
But surely not like a memorial stone in a cemetery,
Or a poppy on Remembrance Sunday?
Has anybody else's command been obeyed
     in quite the same way, Lord?
Your followers have found nothing better:
     for a king at his coronation,
     or a prisoner on the way to die on the scaffold:
     for Parliament having to make important decisions,
     or for schoolchildren taking examinations:
     for Columbus setting out to cross unknown seas,
     or for an old woman afraid to die:
     for astronauts circling the earth,
     or for a bride and groom in a little country church.

And they have done it:
     while the lions roared in their pens,
     waiting for the Christians in the arena;
     on the beaches at Dunkirk in 1940;
     in a Siberian prison camp;
     in splendid cathedrals;
     by a hospital bed;
     at a mother's funeral.
And week by week, all over the world, they are still
     doing it,
Just as you told them to.

Brother Kenneth CSA

Take, Eat

Christ Jesus,
in Holy Communion I find you
under the forms of bread and wine.

In my everyday life I find you
in all the people I meet,
especially when they need help.

For you said,
    Anything you do for one of my brothers
    You do for me.

Mother Teresa of Calcutta

Arrest

(It is 1941, but the Second World War has not yet affected the lives of ten-year-old Esther and her family, who live quietly and happily in the town of Vilna, in Poland.)

The morning it happened – the end of my lovely world – I did not water the lilac bush outside my father's study.

The morning it happened I awakened very early for a reason. Since school was over I was allowed to sleep late. Naturally, in order to enjoy such a special privilege one had to be awake.

The minute I opened my eyes and saw my pink and white curtains fluttering in the soft breeze blowing off the Wilja, I knew it was going to be a beautiful day, a perfect June day. Heeding our family tradition, I was careful to slip out of bed with my right foot forward. Right foot forward, good luck for the day; left foot forward, bad luck. In Poland, one listened to one's family if one wanted good luck.

I went to the window to see if Grandfather was in the garden. This garden was the pride and joy of his life.

That morning, Grandfather was not in the garden. But I leaned out of the window for a minute to admire the roses and the peonies and the lilac bush which I would water in an hour or two I thought.

It must have been about six o'clock.

I picked up the mystery I had been saving for just such a morning, and went back to bed with it.

I was well into the book when my mother burst into the room.

'You must get up immediately,' she said, stripping the bedclothes off me.

'But why? *Mama* –' I was outraged.

'Esther, for once do as you are told without asking questions. Quickly!'

I jumped out of bed.

'Mama – what is it?'

'Questions, always questions. Keep your voice down.' She had dropped hers to a whisper. 'Esther – something is happening. Uncle David called. He said – he said that Russian soldiers were swarming all over Grandfather's apartment. Your father rushed there. He didn't even stop to dress. He's still in his pyjamas. And he isn't back yet. Please get dressed as fast as you can.'

My mother was sitting in the dining-room, at the empty dining-table, resting her chin in her hand.

'Mama, the doorbell is ringing. Don't you hear it? Shall I open the door?'

'No. I shall open it myself.'

She rose slowly and, taking a long time to get there, she opened the door.

My father was on the doorstep, his hands behind his back. Next to him stood two Russian soldiers with fixed bayonets.

Not one word was spoken. Father and Mother exchanged a guarded look, but Father kept his eyes away from me, as if he was ashamed to have me see him in pyjamas with bayonets at his back. Slowly and silently, Father walked through the hall, past the umbrella stand with his walking sticks, into the dining-room. The soldiers walked heavily beside him. When they reached the centre of the room, the silence was broken. One of the soldiers shouted:

'Down on the floor! All of you! You're under arrest!'

Clearly, before we would do such a silly thing, my father would explain everything and the soldiers would go away. He had not done anything wrong – neither stolen, nor killed anyone, nor committed any other crime – they could not arrest him. He would insist that they apologize. But he remained silent. We sat on the floor.

How could we be arrested without having done anything wrong? I decided to find out.

'Why are we under arrest?' I asked.

My mother lifted an admonishing hand, but it was too late.

The soldiers looked to me to my suddenly very pale parents and then at each other. The one who had issued the order had bright little eyes and an extraordinarily broad nose; it was he who pulled out a long white paper and read from it.

'''...you are capitalists and therefore enemies of the people ... you are to be sent to another part of our great and mighty country...'''

The soldier read on and on, the words seeming to pour out of his huge nostrils – so many words and so dull. Most of them were incomprehensible to me. What was a capitalist? The only words that meant anything to me were the ones that were bringing my world to an end. I was to be taken from my home, from the city where I was born, from the people I loved.

My mother spoke quietly. 'Esther, you will go to your room and gather your clothes together.'

I didn't move. Was there to be no argument? no pleading? no miraculous adult intervention?

My mother nudged me and we both scrambled up from the floor. When my father said he would help my mother pack their things and began to get up too, the other soldier tilted his bayonet towards Father and said: 'Don't move. Stay where you are.' My father obeyed, but now he held his head in his hands...

When we walked out of our home into the bright sunshine, I realized that once again I had stepped out with my left foot forward. But this time I knew there was no right foot any place on earth to save us. Only one truck remained and it was waiting for us. It was filled with a blur of silent people. But on the pavement there was a murmur from dozens of curious onlookers. I couldn't understand what they were saying, nor did it matter.

The back door of the truck was bolted and the motor started. The truck began to rumble down Great Pogulanka Avenue, past our white house with its mahogany door – a curtain was blowing out of the dining-room window – past our garden wall, down the avenue where I knew each house, each tree, each chipped stone on the pavement. Beneath my lowered lids I watched my world disappear forever.

I heard our names called hysterically. 'Raya – Samuel – Esther – what is happening? Where are they taking you?' The voice faded, but I recognized my Aunt Sonia racing after the truck with her arms outstretched and her hair flying in the wind. 'Oh, Sonia –' I called out to her and began to sob. My mother pressed my shoulders and softly urged me to stop weeping. I heard some others on the truck also whisper a soft 'Shh... shh...' But I didn't stop; I thought it was time to weep.

Everyone else was quiet. Rumbling past the streets and the green parks and the market place of Vilna, in the bright sunlight they saw their fellow citizens going about their midday business – marketing, pausing to gossip, sunning on a park bench. Witnessing the end of their world, this particular truckload of people were silent.

At the railway station all was confusion: a huge mass of people were milling about; trucks, hundreds of them, were arriving from all directions, each one jammed with people. I searched for a familiar face but saw only the stricken faces of strangers.

Ahead of us the cattle cars were waiting for their human cargo.

Esther Hautzig
(from 'The Endless Steppe')

Arrest

(When Jesus was arrested, someone who saw what happened was a young man called John Mark. He was nearly arrested himself, but managed to escape. He tells Jesus' friends what he saw, from the time that he woke up in the house where Jesus and his disciples had been eating supper earlier that night.)

'…I jumped up in bed with my heart thumping like a drum. I could hear soldiers down below. I heard the rattle of armour and the clink of swords, and rough voices and swearing. I heard their heavy feet go up the staircase and into the top room. I was terribly frightened… One of them called out, "They've escaped!"

'…I don't know now why I did it. I think I meant to warn Jesus. I picked my linen wrap from the side of my bed, and huddled it round me, and followed them…

'I followed them right out of the North Gate, down into the Black Valley. I'd never been there alone before. It was terrible. The Kidron river was tearing along, very nearly in flood, and dark and muddy, and it was so black in there among the trees that you couldn't even see the soldiers, except where the lantern made a red glow here and there. You could hear the clink of their armour, though.

'First we turned left, then we turned right. Then we came to a high wall, and they all stopped. Suddenly I realised where we were. It was the garden of Gethsemane. There was a high wall all round, and inside there were shrubberies of flowering trees. You know the place, don't you? There's a kind of building at the entrance, with an old press for squeezing out oil. That's where we stopped. The soldiers stuck the lantern-poles in the ground. I kept in the shadow, close to the wall.

'Then all at once I saw something that gave me an awful shock. Judas was talking to them! Judas, who'd been at supper in our house!'

'So it was Judas,' said one of the listening men. 'The traitor! We'll kill him for this.'

They were wild with fury. They could hardly listen to Mark's quiet voice.

'I edged up close,' he went on, 'and heard him say, "Is the arrangement quite clear? I'll go straight up and kiss him, as the signal. Then you can close up behind me and take him."…

'I tried to shout. I tried to shout a warning, but my voice stuck in my throat. Then it all seemed to happen at once. I don't quite know what did happen. The soldiers all rushed forward with the lanterns. I could hear people trampling through the trees in every direction. Then I heard them coming back. They were marching back. And they had Jesus in the midst of them, his hands lashed together with ropes. And Judas stood and watched, smiling…'

Nan Goodall
(from 'Donkey's Glory')

Denial

(Peter, the disciple who denied that he knew Jesus, remembers...)

I tell you, Thomas, I think of his suffering every moment of my waking life, and you know why, you know I swore denial of him for fear of it. It was judgment, that night, make no mistake about that. The others tell me that it was there they learnt for the first time how much the Master loved us, or that he invested us with his own authority, or that he gave us the cup of the covenant of the new creation, or I don't know what else. But as for me, he broke my heart that night. The trial came we had been waiting for so long, and what happened? All the treachery, cowardice, faithlessness, lovelessness of our hearts rose to the surface and swamped us. And if they think back, they may remember that early in the meal he said in deep distress, 'One of you, eating here with me, is going to betray me.' And they all said then, 'Is it I?' Those sorrowful words of his cut us to the bone and we all knew just for a moment that we could have been his betrayer. That was what the meal was about, believe me; it was a warning to us of what would happen that night, that evil was at home as well as abroad. He knew what was coming, he knew what was in us, that before another cockcrow one would have betrayed him, the rest all have scattered and left him, and the one who believed he loved him most would have denied before God that he knew him. He tried to tell us that he knew and that in spite of it, it was for us he was laying down his life. So he held the joyful feast of love in the very face of it all, and it was judgment, I tell you, worse than if he had come on the clouds with a sword in his hand.

17

I didn't want to understand. I was uneasy with his strange performance of washing our feet. I told him he should never wash mine, but he looked up at me with that look of his and said, 'If I don't wash you, Peter, you will never be in fellowship with me.' Even then I didn't understand.

He tried to warn me again later, when I was asserting that I was ready to follow him to prison and to death (and the others joined in heartily). 'Peter,' says he, 'before cockcrow you'll have denied me three times.' I said, 'Never! I would lay down my life for you.' Who'd have dreamt it wasn't true? Not I. But: 'Will you indeed?' he says. 'Be careful, Peter! Satan is at work among you. He has been given leave to do his worst. But I've been praying for you, Peter, that your faith may not fail, and when you've come to yourself, you must strengthen your brethren.' It was only later that his words sank in, and I knew he had been praying for me all the time. There and then, I hardly even listened.

He meant us to remember the whole feast, you know. He meant us to think back and understand later. Because it's in the remembering that it hurts, breaks and heals your heart. And why? Because you know then that it was forgiveness all along, that the forsaking and betraying and denying were in that cup he blessed and gave to us. It was his own body and life, that bread and wine, which we were quick enough to swap for a quick getaway. Little did we care for his life then. But he knew we'd be sorry, that we did love him, and that's when we'd remember what he did and know that it was all given back, the love, the fellowship, his life with us, even before we'd given it away. And that's when a body broke down and wept outside the High Priest's house.

There's nothing that hurts worse than forgiveness, there's no burning and purging to equal it. Judas couldn't bear it. He escaped from it through a hanging noose into a place where he thought Jesus could not look at him any more. It's the looking, you know, more than anything.

Believe me, that's what it all meant, the bread and cup and all, and the keeping Passover ahead of time, so that he was killed along with the lambs. He was telling us that this coming death of his was his forgiveness of us and all his other enemies too. He was letting all the worst that was in us come out and have its way on him, so that he could forgive it. I said breaks and heals, didn't I? John has a name for him: he calls him the Bread of Life. So he knows it too.

Was it only for us that that bread was broken? Or did God remember too those kept prisoners so long in their disobedience, from the days of the Flood until now, and all Israel's long, long faith-lessness? Surely that precious blood of forgiveness was ready from the foundation of the world and until the foundations are shaken at the last. Surely all the sinful world must pass through the fire of God's mercy, that I first knew in a cold Jerusalem street as the look of forgiveness from a condemned, betrayed and rejected man.

Caroline Glyn
(from 'In Him Was Life')

Suffering

When Jesus walked through the shopping street
We threw spring flowers before his feet,
Glad to get an excuse to shout,
No need to worry what you shout about.

Chorus:
> *Gentle Christ, wise and good,*
> *We nailed him to a cross of wood.*
> *The Son of God, he lived to save*
> *In a borrowed stable and borrowed grave.*

We looked for a leader to free us from Rome.
We thought we could rule much better at home,
So we welcomed this Saviour with noises and din;
We didn't much want him to free us from sin.
Chorus

Soldiers came at Pilate's call
Led him into the common hall,
Took sharp thorns and made a crown,
Dressed him in a scarlet gown.
Chorus

They spat at him and mocked him then,
Lashed his back again and again,
Laid the cross upon that back,
Forced him up the narrow track.
Chorus

He stumbled through the city gate,
Became too weak to lift the weight,
A man who passed him, black it's said,
Carried up his cross instead.
Chorus

At last they came to the hanging place,
A hill we call the Eyeless Place;
They gave him drugs to kill the pain,
He pushed the cup away again.
Chorus

The soldiers hung him on the cross,
Played for his clothes at pitch and toss.
When each of them had won a share,
Sitting down, they watched him there.
Chorus

They said, as many would say today,
'We wouldn't have treated our Saviour that way'
But gentle Christ, wise and good,
They nailed him to a cross of wood.

> *Gentle Christ, wise and good,*
> *We nailed him to a cross of wood.*
> *The Son of God, he lived to save*
> *In a borrowed stable and borrowed grave.*

Mike Gwilliam
(from 'A Man Dies')

Suffering

At the end of time, billions of people were scattered on a great plain before God's throne. Some of the groups near the front talked heatedly – not with shame before the throne of God, but with embittered anger.

'How can God judge us? How can he know about suffering?' said an angry woman, jerking back her sleeve to reveal a tattooed number from a Nazi concentration camp. 'We endured beatings, terror, torture and death.'

A black man lowered his collar. 'What about this?' he demanded, showing the rope burns. 'Lynched for no crime but being black?'

Hundreds of such groups were visible across the plain. Each had a complaint against God for the evil and suffering he permitted in his world. How lucky God was, they all seemed to agree, able to live in heaven where all is sweetness and light: without weeping, fear, hunger or hatred. What does God know about humanity? What does he know about being forced to endure the pains of life?

So each group sent out a leader, chosen because he had suffered the most. There was a Jew, a black, an untouchable from India, someone from Hiroshima, a Gulag veteran … and others who had known the depths of bitterness and despair. At last they were ready to present their case. It was simple. Before God would be qualified to be their judge, he must endure what they had endured.

Their decision was that God should be sentenced to live on earth as a man … a real man, as helpless as all humanity. They said:

'Let him be a Jew.

Let his birth be in question and his parents refugees.

Let him champion a cause so just, but so radical, that it
brings upon him the hate, condemnation and destructive attacks
of political and religious authorities.

Let him be betrayed and forsaken by his dearest friends.

Let him be indicted on false charges, tried before a
prejudiced jury and convicted by a cowardly judge.

Let him see what it is to be terribly alone and abandoned
by every living being.

Let him be tortured. Let him die.

And let his death be humiliating: let him be jeered at,
mocked, spat on and executed beside common criminals.'

As each leader announced a portion of the sentence, loud murmurs of approval went up from the great throng of people. But suddenly, as the last one had finished pronouncing sentence, there was a long silence. No one moved. They understood the truth.

God had already served his sentence.

Anonymous

Death

(Everyone thought Jamie was clowning around when he fell to the ground after being stung by a bee, even his best friend – who tells the story. But Jamie had a one-in-a-million allergy to bee stings, and he died.)

I sat in the bathtub and poked ripples in the water. Soapy whiskers covered my chin. I hadn't eaten lunch before and now I hadn't eaten supper. Dad and Mom were getting ready to go to the funeral parlour. They asked me if I wanted to go, but I couldn't do that to Jamie. It seemed that as long as I acted like he wasn't dead, he wouldn't be dead.

The ring of ripples broadened, bounced off the sides of the tub and, larger still, came towards me again. Someone said that ripples go on forever and ever, even when you can't see them any more.

I thought of me and Jamie throwing stones in a still pond, watching ripples. Jamie wouldn't make ripples any more. Or shampoo beards.

I grabbed the soap and rubbed up a lather. The soap was my lamp and I was Aladdin. I would rub life back for Jamie. Someone knocked at the door.

'We're going now, sweetheart. We won't be long. If you need anything, you go over to Mrs Mullins.'

They were going. They were going to see Jamie. Suddenly, panicky, I yelled. 'Wait. Wait for me…'

(Jamie lies in his coffin at the undertaker's.)

When I had popped out of the bathtub and said, 'Wait for me,' I hadn't known why. Now I did. I wasn't going to look at him, but if it was possible that Jamie knew what was going on, I wanted him to know that I was here, thinking about him.

There were people all around, talking in whispers, or not talking. Some were crying. I leaned my back against the door frame, thinking of Jamie.

'I'm here. I'm here, Jamie.'

'He looks sweet,' a woman said as she came out of the room. 'Just like he's asleep, bless his heart.'

I remembered how Uncle Jonah looked like he was sleeping. I couldn't imagine Jamie looking like that. I went in and pushed up between my mother and father.

There was Jamie. He was out straight with one hand crossed over his chest. He didn't look like he was asleep to me. Jamie slept all bunched up. Jamie looked dead.

We used to have these staring contests, Jamie and I. We would see who would blink first, or laugh.

It began to sink in that Jamie wasn't going to open his eyes to stare back at me. He wasn't going to blink. He wasn't going to laugh. I ran out of the room and down the hall.

The front yard of the funeral parlour was all green grass and colourful flowers, with lights shining on them. I snatched a yellow bloom from the stem and began tearing it to shreds.

My father called to me and grabbed my shoulder and turned me around ... I buried my head into his chest until the buttons on his suit hurt my face.

Doris Buchanan Smith
(from 'A Taste of Blackberries')

Good Friday

My song is love unknown,
The Saviour's love to me,
Love to the loveless shown,
That they might lovely be.
O, who am I,
That for my sake
My Lord should take
Frail flesh and die?

Sometimes they strew his way,
And his sweet praises sing;
Resounding all the day
Hosannas to their King.
Then 'Crucify!'
Is all their breath,
And for his death
They thirst and cry.

Why, what hath my Lord done?
What makes this rage and spite?
He made the lame to run,
He gave the blind their sight.
Sweet injuries!
Yet they at these
Themselves displease,
And 'gainst him rise.

They rise, and needs will have
My dear Lord made away;
A murderer they save,
The prince of life they slay.
Yet cheerful he
To suffering goes
That he his foes
From thence might free.

In life no house, no home,
My Lord on earth might have;
In death, no friendly tomb,
But what a stranger gave.
What may I say?
Heav'n was his home;
But mine the tomb
Wherein he lay.

Here might I stay and sing,
No story so divine;
Never was love, dear King,
Never was grief like thine.
This is my friend,
In whose sweet praise
I all my days
Could gladly spend.

Samuel Crossman

Good Friday

O King of the Friday

whose limbs were stretched on the cross,

O Lord, who did suffer

the bruises, the wounds, the loss,

we stretch ourselves

beneath the shield of thy might.

May some fruit from the tree of thy Passion

fall on us this night.

Traditional Irish prayer

Giving

(Sara Crewe is rich, the most indulged pupil at her Victorian school for young ladies. But then her father dies penniless; Sara is forced to live in a garret and go half-starved through the cold London streets, doing errands for her cruel headmistress.)

The mud was dreadful – she almost had to wade. She picked her way as carefully as she could, but she could not save herself much; only, in picking her way, she had to look down at her feet and the mud, and in looking down – just as she reached the pavement – she saw something shining in the gutter. It was actually a piece of silver – a tiny piece trodden upon by many feet, but still with spirit enough left to shine a little. Not quite a sixpence, but the next thing to it – a fourpenny piece.

In one second it was in her cold little red-and-blue hand...

And then ... she looked straight at the shop directly facing her. And it was a baker's shop, and a cheerful, stout, motherly woman with rosy cheeks was putting into the window a tray of delicious newly baked hot buns, fresh from the oven – large, plump, shiny buns, with currants in them.

She knew she need not hesitate to use the little piece of money. It had evidently been lying in the mud for some time, and its owner was completely lost in the stream of passing people who crowded and jostled each other all day long.

'But I'll go and ask the baker woman if she has lost anything,' she said to herself rather faintly. So she crossed the pavement and put her wet foot on the step. As she did so she saw something that made her stop.

It was a little figure more forlorn even than herself – a little figure which was not much more than a bundle of rags, from which small, bare, red, muddy feet peeped out, only because the rags with which their owner was trying to cover them were not long enough. Above the rags appeared a shock head of tangled hair, and a dirty face with big, hollow, hungry eyes.

Sara knew they were hungry eyes the moment she saw them, and she felt a sudden sympathy...

'Are you hungry?' she asked.

The child shuffled herself and her rags a little more.

'Ain't I jist?' she said in a hoarse voice. 'Jist ain't I?'...

Just to look at her made Sara feel more hungry and faint...

'Wait a minute,' she said to the beggar child.

She went into the shop. It was warm and smelled deliciously. The woman was just going to put some more hot buns into the window.

'If you please,' said Sara, 'have you lost fourpence – a silver fourpence?' And she held the forlorn little piece of money out to her.

The woman looked at it and then at her... 'Bless us, no!' she answered. 'Did you find it?'

'Yes,' said Sara. 'In the gutter.'

'Keep it, then,' said the woman. 'It may have been there for a week, and goodness knows who lost it. You could never find out.'

'I know that,' said Sara, 'but I thought I would ask you.'

'Not many would,' said the woman, looking puzzled and good-natured all at once.

'Do you want to buy something?' she added, as she saw Sara glance at the buns.

'Four buns, if you please,' said Sara. 'Those at a penny each.'

The woman went to the window and put some in a paper bag. Sara noticed that she put in six.

'I said four, if you please,' she explained. 'I have only fourpence.'

'I'll throw in two for makeweight,' said the woman, with her good-natured look. 'I dare say you can eat them sometime. Aren't you hungry?'

A mist rose before Sara's eyes.

'Yes,' she answered, 'I am very hungry, and I am much obliged to you for your kindness; and – ' she was going to add – 'there is a child outside who is hungrier than I am.' But just at that moment two or three customers came in at once…

The beggar girl was still huddled up in the corner of the step. She looked frightful in her wet and dirty rags. She was staring straight before her with a stupid look of suffering…

Sara opened the paper bag and took out one of the hot buns, which had already warmed her own cold hands a little.

'See,' she said, putting the bun in the ragged lap,' this is nice and hot. Eat it, and you will not feel so hungry.'

The child started and stared up at her, as if such sudden, amazing good luck almost frightened her; then she snatched up the bun and began to cram it into her mouth with great wolfish bites.

'Oh, my! Oh, my!' Sara heard her say hoarsely, in wild delight. 'Oh, *my!*'

Sara took out three more buns and put them down.

The sound in the hoarse, ravenous voice was awful.

'She is hungrier than I am,' she said to herself. 'She's starving.' But her hand trembled when she put down the fourth bun. 'I'm not starving,' she said – and she put down the fifth.

Frances H. Burnett
(from 'A Little Princess')

(After Sara has gone, the baker woman, 'feeling more disturbed in her comfortable mind than she has done for many a day', calls the beggar child into the warmth and feeds her, 'for that young one's sake'.)

Giving

Said Judas to Mary
'Now what will you do
With your ointment
So rich and so rare?'
'I'll pour it all over
The feet of the Lord
And I'll wipe it away with my hair,'
                    She said
'I'll wipe it away with my hair.'

'Oh Mary, Oh Mary,
Oh think of the poor –
This ointment, it
Could have been sold.
And think of the blankets
And think of the bread
You could buy with the silver and gold,'
                    He said
'You could buy with the silver and gold.'

'Tomorrow, tomorrow,
I'll think of the poor
Tomorrow' she said
'Not today,
For dearer than all
Of the poor in the world
Is my love who is going away,'
                    She said
'My love who is going away.'

Said Jesus to Mary
'Your love is so deep
Today you may do
As you will.
Tomorrow you say
I am going away.
But my body I leave with you still,'
                    He said
'My body I leave with you still.'

'The poor of the world
Are my body' He said,
'To the end of the world they shall be.
The bread and the blankets
You give to the poor
You'll find you have given to me,'
                              He said
'You'll find you have given to me.'

'My body will hang
On the cross of the world
Tomorrow,' He said
'And today,
And Martha and Mary
Will find me again
And wash all my sorrow away,'
                              He said
'And wash all my sorrow away.'

Sydney Carter

Love

Tomorrow shall be my dancing day;
I would my true love did so chance
To see the legend of my play,
To call my true love to my dance.
        Sing O my love, my love, my love –
        This have I done for my true love.

In a manger laid and wrapt I was,
So very poor, this was my chance.
Betwixt an ox and a silly poor ass,
To call my true love to my dance.
        Sing O my love, my love, my love –
        This have I done for my true love.

Into the desert I was led,
Where I fasted without substance,
The devil bade me make stones my bread,
To have me break my true love's dance.
        Sing O my love, my love, my love –
        This have I done for my true love.

For thirty pence Judas me sold
His covetousness for to advance:
'Mark who I kiss, the same do hold',
The same is he shall lead the dance.
        Sing O my love, my love, my love –
        This have I done for my true love.

Then on a cross hanged I was,
Where a spear to my heart did glance;
There issued forth both water and blood,
To call my true love to the dance.
        Sing O my love, my love, my love –
        This have I done for my true love.

Then down to Hell I took my way
For my true love's deliverance,
And rose again on the third day
Up to my true love and the dance.
        Sing O my love, my love, my love –
        This have I done for my true love.

Traditional

Love bade me welcome, yet my soul drew back,
    Guilty of dust and sin.
But quick-eyed Love, observing me grow slack
    From my first entrance in,
Drew nearer to me, sweetly questioning
    If I lacked any thing.

'A guest', I answered, 'worthy to be here.'
    Love said, 'You shall be he.'
'I, the unkind, the ungrateful? Ah, my dear,
    I cannot look on thee.'
Love took my hand, and smiling did reply,
    'Who made the eyes but I?'

'Truth, Lord, but I have marred them; let my shame
    Go where it doth deserve.'
'And know you not', says Love, 'who bore the blame?'
    'My dear, then I will serve.'
'You must sit down,' says Love, 'and taste my meat.'
    So I did sit and eat.

George Herbert

Following

I am going to Calvary.
Would you like to come with me
all the way and back again?
You must follow the leader then –
       you must follow the leader,
       you must follow the leader,
       all the way and back again
       you must follow the leader.

If I wear a thorny crown,
if the soldiers knock me down
can I really be a king? –
Love will answer everything,
       if you follow the leader,
       if you follow the leader,
       love will answer everything
       if you follow the leader.

When I go along the road,
I shall lift a heavy load.
I will carry a cross for you.
You will learn to carry it too
       if you follow the leader,
       if you follow the leader,
       you will learn to carry it too
       if you follow the leader

I am going to climb a hill
where the soldiers wait to kill.
Soldiers, let me pray for you.
Love can bear the wrongs you do,
       when you follow the leader,
       when you follow the leader,
       love can bear the wrongs you do
       when you follow the leader.

I am going to stretch my hands,
reaching out to all the lands.
Can I really be a king? –
Love's the lord of everything,
        when you follow the leader,
        when you follow the leader,
        love's the lord of everything
        when you follow the leader.

I have come from Calvary.
Now the world can live with me.
All the way and back again
you can follow the leader then –
        you can follow the leader,
        you can follow the leader,
        all the way and back again
        you can follow the leader.

Brian Wren

Rescue

(The clockwork mouse and his child, escaping from a wicked rat, have been tipped from a makeshift raft into a pond, and have sunk to the bottom, together with their brass good-luck coin. There they meet a sad, ugly little creature, 'something like a misshapen grasshopper' called Miss Mudd, and see the big fish called bass.)

Hours passed, and it was midday when Miss Mudd's ugly little face appeared among the reeds and lily pads where the nutshell drum (belonging to the mouse's child) still floated quietly by the edge of the pond. She clung tiredly to the reed stem she had climbed, a length of fishing line hanging straight down from her jaws into the water. With what seemed the last of her strength she hauled up the end of the line with the good-luck coin attached... Now, although it was not bright, the brass was capable of glimmering in the water, and she hoped it would suffice... Dragging it on to a lily pad, Miss Mudd left it there among the loose coils of line, then climbed down the reed stem and disappeared below the surface.

In an hour or so she reappeared, more line in her jaws, on the rocks near the bank, where a row of painted turtles lay basking in the sun. Risking her life as she passed each turtle, Miss Mudd crept stealthily on until she came to a flat rock overhung by the low branches of the sumac on the bank. Here she dragged the line through a narrow fork in one of the branches, then staggered on across the lily pads to where the nutshell drum still rocked in the ripples among the reeds. Working more and more slowly, she tied the end of the line to the strap of the drum. Then she took the end of the line coiled on the lily pad, tied it also to the drum strap, and pushed the coin into the water. The nutshell drum went under, then bobbed up again. Peering down through the water, Miss Mudd saw the coin swinging below her, its worn brass gleaming faintly, like a forlorn hope.

'There,' she said, 'that's it,' and she collapsed, exhausted, on the lily pad. 'I feel so odd!' she said. 'I can scarcely catch my breath, and my eyes are growing dim. Perhaps I'm dying, and my little muddy life is finished, and I never was meant to be anything but what I was.'

Miss Mudd began to cry, and as her body heaved it split down the back. 'Oh!' she said, and felt the life stir in her wet and wrinkled wings that were already stiffening for flight. 'It was so difficult to be sure!' she sighed. She climbed out of the empty, muddy shell of her discarded self, a dragonfly now, new and lovely, emerald green. She waited patiently until the sun had dried her iridescent wings, then launched herself uncertainly to fly... Glittering over the pond she flew away, lilting on the warm wind like a song in the sunlight, like a sigh in the summer air.

In the mud at the bottom, the mouse and his child waited ... Serpentina (*the turtle*) awoke, yawned, and snapped his jaws hungrily.

'One rises afresh,' he said, 'to new investigations of TO BE. What have you found beyond the farther side of nothing?'

'A way out,' replied the mouse child.

'Indeed!' said Serpentina. 'Have you paused to consider that there *is* no way out? Each way out of one situation necessarily being the way into another situation, we may say that – Stop! Pay attention!'

But the mouse and his child, exploding from a cloud of mud, were half-way to the sunlit surface of the pond. Above them, the nutshell drum went slanting down into the water. The bass that had swallowed the coin was off like a bullet, and the line cut a V-shaped wake through the water as it ran smoking over the forked branch and hauled up the long-submerged tin mice.

Sodden and heavy with the silt of the bottom, they broke the surface, burst splashing into the sunlight, and went skittering across the turtle rocks... The mouse and his child lay in a puddle on the stone as the water drained out of them. They were spotted, streaked, and pitted with rust at all their joints, and the arms they stretched out to each other were naked, rusty wires... The sunlight seemed intolerably bright, and its warmth on their tin was delightful. Sounds were needle-sharp and clear; they listened to the rustling of the leaves...

Russell Hoban
(from 'The Mouse and his Child')

Rescue

(The young monk Niall and Princess Finnglas are trapped between the angry crew of King Kernac's warship, in which they are trying to escape, and a crowd of furiously hostile villagers. With them is Pangur Ban, the white cat, who was once told by the huge, laughing, powerful dolphin, Arthmael: 'Learn, Pangur Ban, that I will always come when you need me. Though you, of all creatures, will wish you had never called.' Pangur falls into the river and is tangled in a salmon net.)

'Help!' screamed Pangur. 'Don't leave me to drown!'

And the very last woman at the back of the crowd heard him.

She turned and ran back to the river-bank, peering over. Her shout of triumph went ringing over the beach.

'The white cat! The Unlucky One! He's here! We've got him!'

The crowd's anger turned from the sea. They came surging back towards the salmon net, hatred in their faces. They had sticks raised in their hands. Stones seized from the beach.

'Kill him! Kill him!'

'Help!' wailed Pangur in pure terror. *'Arthmael! Help me!'*

A great cloud darkened the sun. Out of the indigo sea, like a bolt of lightning, a white wave-wash came streaking between the rocks, storming past the stolen ship, tossing the swimming warriors aside, furrowing the still water of the bay, charging towards the salmon-net and the snared Pangur.

He saw the blue-black snout rushing towards him. No laughter in the bottle-nosed face now. No twinkle in the round bright eye. A fierce, fixed, unswervable, unstoppable tempest of deliverance.

'Arthmael!' he cried. 'Arthmael! Save me!'

Fay Sampson
(from 'Pangur Ban, the White Cat')

Sacrifice

(Arthmael, the great dolphin, has come to the rescue of Pangur Ban, the white cat, who is trapped in a salmon net at the mercy of a murderous crowd. Pangur's friends, Niall and Finnglas, are helpless aboard their ship.)

A yell broke from the crowd on the bank above them.

'He's freeing the cat!'

'He's breaking the net!'

'Kill the sea-devil!'

Their raised clubs darkened the sky like a thunder-cloud, and fell. The dolphin's great head arched over the little white cat, shielding him from the blows. Again and again the sharp white teeth bit into the net... The blizzard of white water was flecked with pink. Beneath it, desperate, grim as Pangur had never seen him before, Arthmael's jaws bit and bit again in a race against death...

He could see nothing but Arthmael's white underbelly. He was safe beneath it. Then the last strand parted from his tangled paw and he felt the current take him...

'Arthmael...'

'Go!' roared Arthmael, with his jaws full of net. 'Go, and be thankful!'

He was moving faster now, slipping, spinning down the stream. He was out in the open bay. He was swimming. He turned his head.

'Arthmael?'

He glimpsed a great fountain of spray in the river-mouth. Then the jade-green waves rose higher than his head, blossoming with bubbles of rose-red foam as though the sun was setting.

'Arthmael!' called Pangur. But his thin wail rose and lost itself in the empty sky. He was alone.

Hands scooped him from the water. With a gasp he opened his eyes and found himself on Niall's lap. he shook his wet fur and pressed against him, purring. But the monk's hands dropped away from him. He was staring at the shore. Finnglas had lowered the sail. She too was staring at the river-mouth. A terrible silence gripped the warship.

Across the beach the crowd was thickening every moment, black as swarming bees. On the river-bank stones were flying, clubs rising and falling, swords lifting against the sky. Over and over again...

'We've got to go back and save him!' cried Finnglas. She grabbed the steering-ar.

Niall's hand closed over her wrist. He pointed down at the water.

'It's too late. We must save ourselves now. Look.'

The first pink flecks of foam were touching the ship, like chaffinch feathers. But out of the river a stronger stream was flowing. Bright red, streaking the turquoise water like sunset at noon...

'They're *killing* him!' whispered Pangur unbelievingly. 'They're killing Arthmael!'

'He *can't* die!' shouted Finnglas. 'He saved us all. Arthmael can't die!'

But his blood was staining the bay like a funeral fire.

A savage shout of triumph rose from the shore.

'It is finished,' breathed Finnglas, wide-eyed.

'He was Arthmael, the Clown, the great Dancer,' muttered Niall. 'When he dies, the dance is over.'

Fay Sampson
(from 'Pangur Ban, the White Cat')

Repentance

(Lucy, Edmund and their spoilt, quarrelsome cousin Eustace are aboard the *Dawn Treader*, sailing the seas beyond Narnia, the land whose guardian is the great, mysterious lion Aslan. On an island Eustace discovers a dragon's cave, tries on a gold bracelet and goes to sleep on the dragon's treasure. But in the morning he has turned into a dragon, and nothing that his friends can do will help him.)

About six days after they had landed on Dragon Island, Edmund happened to wake up very early one morning... Presently he thought he saw a dark figure moving on the seaward side of the wood... Edmund drew his sword and was about to challenge the stranger when the stranger said in a low voice, 'Is that you, Edmund? ... Don't you know me? It's me – Eustace.'

...They went to the rocks and sat down looking out across the bay while the sky got paler and paler and the stars disappeared except for one very bright one low down and near the horizon.

'I won't tell you how I became a – a dragon till I can tell the others and get it all over,' said Eustace... 'I want to tell you how I stopped being one... Well, last night I was more miserable than ever. And that beastly arm-ring was hurting like anything –'

Eustace laughed – a different laugh from any Edmund had heard him give before – and slipped the bracelet easily off his arm. 'There it is,' he said, 'and anyone who likes can have it as far as I'm concerned. Well, as I say, I was lying awake and wondering what on earth would become of me. And then – but, mind you, it may have been all a dream. I don't know.'

'Go on,' said Edmund with considerable patience.

'Well, anyway, I looked up and saw the very last thing I expected: a huge lion coming slowly towards me ... I was terribly afraid of it. Well, it came close up to me and looked straight into my eyes. And I shut my eyes tight. But that wasn't any good because it told me to follow it.'

'You mean it spoke?'

'I don't know. Now that you mention it, I don't think it did. But it told me all the same... And it led me a long way into the mountains. So at last we came to the top of a mountain I'd never seen before and on the top of this mountain there was a garden – trees and fruit and everything. In the middle of it there was a well.

'I knew it was a well because you could see the water bubbling up from the bottom of it: but it was a lot bigger than most wells – like a big round bath with marble steps going down into it. The water was as clear as anything and I thought if I could get in there and bathe it would ease the pain in my leg. But the lion told me I must undress first. Mind you, I don't know if he said any words out loud or not.

'I was just going to say that I couldn't undress because I hadn't any clothes on when I suddenly thought that dragons are snaky sort of things and snakes can cast their skins... So I started scratching myself and my scales began coming off all over the place. And then I scratched a little deeper and instead of just scales coming off here and there, my whole skin started peeling off beautifully, like it does after an illness, or as if I were a banana. In a minute or two I just stepped out of it. I could see it lying there beside me, looking rather nasty. It was a most lovely feeling. So I started to go down into the well for my bathe.

'But just as I was going to put my feet into the water I looked down and saw that they were all hard and rough and wrinkled and scaly just as they had been before. Oh, that's all right, said I, it only means I had another smaller suit on underneath the first one, and I'll have to get out of it too... Well, exactly the same thing happened again... So I scratched away for the third time and got off a third skin, just like the two others, and stepped out of it. But as soon as I looked at myself in the water I knew it had been no good.

'Then the lion said – but I don't know if it spoke – ''You will have to let me undress you.'' I was afraid of his claws, I can tell you, but I was pretty desperate now. So I just lay flat down on my back to let him do it.

'The very first tear he made was so deep that I thought it had gone right into my heart. And when he began pulling the skin off, it hurt worse than anything I've ever felt. The only thing that made me able to bear it was just the pleasure of feeling the stuff peel off. You know – if you've ever picked the scab off a sore place... Well, he peeled the beastly stuff right off – just as I thought I'd done it myself the other three times, only they hadn't hurt -- and there it was lying on the grass: only ever so much thicker, and darker, and more knobbly-looking than the others had been... Then he caught hold of me – I didn't like that much for I was very tender underneath now that I'd no skin on – and threw me into the water. It smarted like anything but only for a moment. After that it became perfectly delicious and as soon as I started swimming and splashing I found that all the pain had gone from my arm. And then I saw why. I'd turned into a boy again... And then suddenly I was back here. Which is what makes me think it must have been a dream.'

'It wasn't a dream,' said Edmund... 'I think you've seen Aslan.'

C. S. Lewis
(from 'The Voyage of the Dawn Treader')

Repentance

Lord, when did we see you?

I was hungry and starving
       and you were obese;
Thirsty
       and you were watering your garden;
With no road to follow and without hope
       and you called the police
       and were happy that they took me prisoner;
Barefoot and with ragged clothing
       and you were saying, 'I have nothing
       to wear, tomorrow I must buy something new';
Sick
       and you asked, 'Is it infectious?';
Prisoner
       and you said, 'That's where people like you
       should be!'

Lord, have mercy.

Anonymous

Morning

The horns of the morning
Are blowing, are shining,
The meadows are bright
    With the coldest dew;
The dawn reassembles.
Like the clash of gold cymbals
The sky spreads its vans out
    The sun hangs in view.

Here, where no love is,
All that was hopeless
And kept me from sleeping
    Is frail and unsure;
For never so brilliant,
Neither so silent
Nor so unearthly, has
    Earth grown before.

Philip Larkin

New Life

(Charlotte the spider, who saved Wilbur the pig from being sold, has died – but Wilbur is watching over the sac which contains Charlotte's eggs.)

All winter Wilbur watched over Charlotte's egg sac as though he were guarding his own children. He had scooped out a special place in the manure for the sac, next to the board fence. On very cold nights he lay so that his breath would warm it. For Wilbur, nothing in life was so important as this small round object – nothing else mattered. Patiently he awaited the end of the winter and the coming of the little spiders. Life is always a rich and steady time when you are waiting for something to happen or to hatch. The winter ended at last.

'I heard the frogs,' said the old sheep one evening. 'Listen! You can hear them now.'

Wilbur stood still and cocked his ears. From the pond, in shrill chorus, came the voices of hundreds of little frogs.

'Springtime,' said the old sheep, thoughtfully. 'Another spring.' As she walked away, Wilbur saw a new lamb following her. It was only a few hours old.

The snows melted and ran away. The streams and ditches bubbled and chattered with rushing water. A sparrow with a streaky breast arrived and sang. The light strengthened, the mornings came sooner. Almost every morning there was another lamb in the sheepfold. The goose was sitting on nine eggs. The sky seemed wider and a warm wind blew. The last remaining strands of Charlotte's old web floated away and vanished.

One fine sunny morning, after breakfast, Wilbur stood watching his precious sac. He wasn't thinking of anything much. As he stood there, he noticed something move. He stepped closer and stared. A tiny spider crawled from the sac. It was no bigger than the head of a pin. Its body was grey with a black stripe underneath. It looked just like Charlotte.

Wilbur trembled all over when he saw it. The little spider waved at him. Then Wilbur looked more closely. Two more little spiders crawled out and waved. They climbed round and round on the sac, exploring their new world. Then three more little spiders. Then eight. Then ten. Charlotte's children were here at last.

Wilbur's heart pounded. He began to squeal. Then he raced in circles, kicking manure into the air. Then he turned a back flip. Then he planted his front feet and came to a stop in front of Charlotte's children.

'Hello there!' he said...

E. B. White
(from 'Charlotte's Web')

Resurrection

(This 'hymn of the Resurrection' was written about 1500 and has been adapted into modern English, but keeping as closely to the original as possible. The last line of each verse means 'The Lord has risen from the tomb'.)

Done is a battle on the dragon black!
Our champion, Christ, confounded has his foes;
The gates of hell are broken with a crack;
The sign triumphal raised is of the Cross;
The devils tremble with a hideous voice;
The souls are freed and into bliss can go;
Christ with his blood our ransom does endorse;
Surrexit Dominus de sepulchro.

Downed is the deadly dragon, Lucifer,
The cruel serpent with the mortal sting,
The old, keen tiger with his teeth ajar,
Who in a wait has lain for us so long,
Thinking to grip us in his claws so strong:
The merciful Lord would not that it were so –
He made him for to fail in that desire.
Surrexit Dominus de sepulchro.

He for our sake that suffered to be slain
And like a lamb in sacrifice was dight,
Is like a lion risen up again
And as a giant stretches his full height.
Up is Aurora, radiant and bright,
Aloft is gone the glorious Apollo;
The blissful day has parted from the night.
Surrexit Dominus de sepulchro.

William Dunbar

('dight' means to lay out or dress; Aurora was the Greek goddess of the dawn, Apollo the god of the sun.)

Resurrection

(Niall, Finnglas and Pangur Ban sail away after the death of the dolphin Arthmael and land on an island, where they find Drusticc, Abbess of the monastery from which Niall was banished long ago.)

One name they could not speak, because his loss was more than they could bear. Pangur crouched at Drusticc's feet on the damp seaweed and mewed piteously.

She picked him up and he buried his face in her robe.

'You don't know,' he wailed. 'You don't know the worst thing of all. It was my fault. I have killed Arthmael!'

He felt Drusticc tremble.

'He died to save me. *Me?* I wasn't worth it!'

'But you are worth it to him, Pangur Ban, because he loved you.'

'I'd do anything to bring him back. *Anything.* But there is nothing I can do, is there? It is all over.'

Her chest was quivering now. Over his head her voice broke into ringing laughter as she turned him round to face the world.

'Oh, Pangur Ban! Did you think you could silence the great Clown, the Dancer? Did you think your little sin could put out the light of the world? Will you look there!'

A single shaft of sunlight struck down through the mist. They saw no land but, where it touched the water, waves broke against a rock. Around it, a glittering circle began to grow, brighter and brighter, till they could hardly bear to look at it... The watchers held their breath.

The great, scarred dolphin leaped straight up out of the ocean. The swift, blue-black length of him arched across the sun. It gilded the yellow streak along his side, silvered his flashing belly, made diamonds of his laughing eyes. He dived with an almighty splash. The waves of his leaping washed over their feet. Then his strong tail lashed once, lifting his joyful face to the world again.

'Arthmael!'

Pangur squirmed to leap free, to run to him.

'Not yet!' Drusticc's command rang out... Then, more gently, 'Wait, Pangur Ban. Your turn will come.'

And in the midst of the laughter and the leaping, Arthmael sprang up on his tail and danced for them...

Then, for the last time, Arthmael leaped from under the sea. Powering up through all the layers of creation. Soaring on into the sky and the sun.

The watchers gazed upwards till their eyes were dazzled, and they had to blink and turn away. When they looked again, the mist had closed upon the bay. But overhead the sun was strengthening.

Fay Sampson
(from 'Pangur Ban, the White Cat')

Victory

(Raymond, who is seriously ill – indeed, though he does not know it, he is not going to get better – has been given a new record.)

The record had a funny title, Haydn's 'Concerto for Trumpet and Orchestra in E Flat'. Haydn must be the name of the composer – it couldn't be the name of a group because Ben had said that it wasn't a pop record...

At first he was a little disappointed. The orchestra was quite pleasant, but it was mainly violins, which he always thought were rather squeaky instruments, and there didn't seem to be any definite tune. But then, suddenly and unexpectedly, but yet (Raymond thought) just at the right moment, the trumpet came through on its own, playing a clear, confident, bold tune which, he could now see, had been present in the opening part played by the violins all the time. The tune was rich and thrilling, and the trumpeter seemed to be enjoying himself as he skated up and down the scales, scattering his silver notes in all directions.

But now things became even more exciting, because the rest of the orchestra came back in, and a kind of duel developed between the trumpeter and all the other instruments, each trying to seize and hold on to the tune in turn and to do more daring and difficult things with it. It was more than a duel – it was battle in which one man seemed to be taking on a whole army single-handed...

And now a really extraordinary thing happened. The trumpeter, by sheer skill and courage and persistence, forced all the rest of the orchestra into silence and for several seconds, or minutes – it seemed to Raymond almost like an eternity – he did exactly as he pleased, swooping and darting and curving and soaring and pirouetting in a marvellous one-man display of trumpet technique, climbing daringly up to heights that made Raymond hold his breath for fear the note would crack or waver then suddenly plunging down to depths that Raymond had imagined only the tuba or the trombone could reach. And then, just at the moment when the trumpeter's conquest was complete, he brought the tune back to the orchestra, and they all joined in joyfully together, so that what had seemed like a victory for one instrument alone became in the end a victory for them all.

As the record clicked off and Raymond lay back on his pillow (for he had been sitting bolt upright in sheer astonishment), he felt that he understood what that music had been saying to him. But he couldn't put it into words, and he didn't even try to. He just felt filled with peace – the kind of peace that comes just at the moment of achieving something very difficult or very dangerous.

Colin Wood
(from 'The Alabama Story')

Liberation

Universe
and every universe beyond,
spin and blaze,
whirl and dance,
leap and laugh
as never before.
It's happened
It's new
It's here.
The liberation.
The victory.
The new creation.
Christ has smashed death.
He has liberated the world.
He has freed the universe.
You and I and everything
are free again,
alive again.

Let's have a festival
and follow him across the skies,
through the flames of heaven
and back down every alley of our town.
There, let's have him come
to liberate our city,
clean up the mess
and start all over again.
You conquered.
Keep on fighting through us.
You arose.
Keep on rising in us.

You celebrated.
Keep on celebrating with us.
You happen.
You are new.
You are here.

Norman C. Habel
(from 'Interrobang')

Word

(The first verses of chapter 1 of St John's Gospel are the inspiration for this hymn. They tell us that the world is not an accident; its creation was and is rooted in the will and Word of God, who came to us as Jesus, 'true God and true man'.)

Before the world began,
One Word was there;
Grounded in God he was,
Rooted in care;
By him all things were made,
In him was love displayed,
Through him God spoke, and said,
'I AM FOR YOU'.

Life found in him its source,
Death found its end;
Light found in him its course,
Darkness its friend.
For neither death nor doubt
Nor darkness can put out
The glow of God, the shout,
'I AM FOR YOU'.

The Word was in the world
Which from him came;
Unrecognised he was,
Unknown by name.
One with all humankind,
With the unloved aligned,
Convincing sight and mind,
'I AM FOR YOU'.

All who received the Word
By God were blessed;
Sisters and brothers they
Of earth's fond guest.
So did the Word of Grace
Proclaim in time and space
And with a human face,
'I AM FOR YOU'.

John Bell and Graham Maule
(from 'Wild Goose Songs')

50
Lord, stretch our minds.
Make us think, Lord.
Prick us to look again
at the phrases that trip off our tongues in church
and see them with fresh eyes.
Make us alive
to the huge things we say and sing.
When we are letting familiar words wash over us,
wake us up to the enormity
of what they are telling us.
Lord, what you are and what you have done
are more than our little brains can properly get hold of.
But stimulate us
at least to make the effort.

David Jenkins
(from 'Further Everyday Prayers')

Easter

(A true account, by a visiting American, of the service held on Easter Eve in a Russian Orthodox church in the late 1980s.)

Kiev, Easter, April 19:
'Christos Voskresey! Veyeastino voskresey!' Christ is risen! Truly he is risen! I have heard and exchanged these words countless times in the past twelve hours, so often that the words seem to say themselves.

Just after ten, Boris, Volodya and I drove out to Boris' parish church, Our Lady of the Protecting Veil, a brick church built in 1906 that stands on a hilltop on the west edge of Kiev. Though it was still half an hour before the service was due to start, there was a steady stream of people walking up the dark hillside. A policeman stood at the foot of the hill blocking the way to cars. An exception was made for us but only when the driver promised to bring the car back down after dropping us off.

Though it isn't a large church, there were at least two thousand people jammed inside and as many around the church. Boris thought it best to put me on the altar side of the iconostasis *(the tall screen hung with holy pictures)* where there was space and also a few chairs. I was, at first, disappointed. A true Russian Easter is spent standing in the crowd, not on the altar side of the iconostasis. But after the first hour I realised I wouldn't have lasted through the service otherwise.

I was near the centre of the iconostasis, next to the Royal Doors *(leading to the altar)*, where I had a view of tables heaped with Easter bread – *kulich* – in the foreground and a sea of faces illumined by candlelight.

The people who stood out the most from my vantage point were a group of lanky teenagers who had apparently never been in church before – 'window-shoppers,' Volodya whispered to me. They didn't cross themselves, didn't bow, but behaved like passive spectators at a play. The women didn't wear scarves. The tallest, a young woman, looked like her Dutch counterparts – short blonde hair cut in punkish style standing up from her head, and blue-shadowed eyes. The most striking thing about her was her alert eyes, round as saucers, watching everything with awe. Now and then she pointed out to her boyfriend something that had caught her attention. There was real excitement in her face, a deep engagement. Perhaps one day I will return here and find her wearing a scarf and crossing herself.

Actually it wasn't Easter when the service began. Lent had another hour to run. Easter began with a sung announcement of the resurrection. The dean went out the royal doors into the congregation and sang out, *'Christos voskresey!'* Everyone responded in one voice, *'Veyeastino voskresey!'* It is impossible to put on paper how this sounds in the dead of night in a church overheated by crowds of people and hundreds of candles. It is like a shudder in the earth, the cracking open of a tomb. Then there was an explosion of bell-ringing. Russian bells sing their own Easter hymn in a particular pattern of sound that rejoices in the victory of life over death.

The congregation, singing an Easter hymn, followed the priests out of the church and circled the building in a slow procession. Those already outside, holding candles in their hands, parted to make way for the procession. The singing was continuous. All the while the bells were sounding out for miles around, in the deepest night, the news of the resurrection.

Finally the procession came back into the church. Once again there was hardly room to breathe. The priests arranged themselves in front of the iconostasis and sang the opening five verses of the Gospel according to St. John:

'In the beginning was the Word, and the Word was with God, and the Word was God. He was in the beginning with God. All things were made through him and without him was not anything made that was made. In him was life and the life was the light of men. The light shines in the darkness and the darkness has not overcome it.'

This was done first in Church Slavonic, then in seven other languages: Ukrainian, Russian, Greek, Latin, English, French and German. More languages would have been used if they were known to any of the priests. 'The more languages we use in singing the Easter Gospel,' Volodya said to me, 'the better we like it. I was in a Moscow church where they sang the Gospel in twelve languages. It makes the whole world present.'

After the five-hour service – vespers, Easter proclamation, morning prayer, Eucharist – the crowd outside parted to form a pathway about two yards wide which was lined with baskets full of food, each basket dominated by the Easter bread and lit by a candle struggling against the wind. There was still no hint of dawn in the sky. A priest lavishly dowsed every basket with water blessed at the Easter service, at the same time showering everything and everyone. So many people were there to have their Easter baskets blessed that the circles kept reforming. It took more than an hour for the four priests, working in turns, to bless every basket.

Even then the night was far from over. Next came a big meal. While the congregation walked back to the tables in their own homes, the priests and staff of the parish went into an old one-storey wooden building that clung precariously to the edge of the hill, the parish house, where meat and home-made sausage and Easter eggs and Easter bread awaited us.

We remained at the table until about 8 o'clock in the morning. It wasn't only food but drink – vodka, wine, Russian soft drinks and

Pepsi Cola (the brand name in cyrillic letters and the contents bottled under US licence in the USSR). There were many toasts, including some to me and some to world peace, which I momentarily represented.

At some point I looked at all these men and women crowded around the table, laughing and telling stories, and found myself overcome by love for them, and stunned at the thought that they would be likely casualties in another world war. One of the people at the table was the choir director, who wore a well-tailored suit and had the look of an old English gentleman. Perhaps because he found out I sing in a choir and that two of my sons do also, there was a particular sense of connection between us. Before we parted this older man wept on my shoulder. I cried as well.

I wrote a message in the parish guest book. It has been little written in since it was started in 1974. The last entry before mine was from a group of British pilgrims that came to Kiev in 1984. Then I was given several loaves of Easter bread, a sack of beautifully coloured Easter eggs and an armful of flowers. As we left, I noticed people were already arriving for the morning service. The dawn had broken.

Utterly exhausted, Volodya and I went back to the hotel to sleep, but before going to my room I gave the woman at the desk on our floor some of the Easter eggs and one of the loaves of Easter bread. Overcoming worry that a religious greeting might offend her, I said, 'Christos Voskresey!' She smiled and replied, 'Veyeastino voskresey!'

Jim Forrest
(from 'Finding God among the Russians')

Easter

(A carol for Holy Week, to the tune of 'The Twelve Days of Christmas'.)

On the day of Good Friday
My true love gave to me
His own self upon a bare tree.

On the Saturday that followed
My true love gave to me
Rest after pain
And his own self upon a bare tree.

On the first day of Easter
My true love gave to me
Life, new life,
Rest after pain
And his own self upon a bare tree.

All the day after Easter
My true love gives to me
Grace for my living,
Joy in my giving,
Comfort in sorrow,
Strength for tomorrow,
Love without end –
His risen light,
Life, new life,
Rest after pain
And his own self upon a bare tree.

Pamela Egan

Acceptance

Perhaps the greatest of all the musical masterpieces which speak of transformation is *The Magic Flute*. There is fear in the opera, but it is cast out by perfect love; there is temptation, but it is resisted with the aid of a power which never fails; there are ordeals to endure, but they are accepted as part of the journey from this world to another; there is evil, but it is overcome by good.

Many years ago, I dreamed that I was talking to a group of people who were about to set off on holiday; they were staying, they told me, with a most hospitable man in his most beautiful house, and there would be many others there. Why, they asked, did not I come too? I protested that I hardly knew *them*, and their host not at all – how could I possibly impose myself on him! Nonsense, they replied, he would welcome me as he welcomed everybody, whether known to him nor not. I went along, tormented by the fear of being rejected when I arrived, especially if everyone else was allowed in.

We arrived by water; there was a huge crowd on the boat, and more crowds on the shore, all making for the same paragon of hospitality. The more impatient leaped to the shore; some missed their footing and fell between boat and ground, but it made no difference, for they all still landed safely, intact but sprawling, greeted by a wave of happy laughter from those already on firm ground. I made my way cautiously down the gangway, ashamed of my cowardice, but fell none the less as I stepped ashore; I was not hurt, but I, too, was engulfed in laughter, and the laughter, I found, did not hurt either.

We arrived at the house; all was as I had been promised. Crowds mingled in vast rooms bathed in light, all with vast windows looking on to beautiful scenery. Our benign host pressed us to eat, to drink, to be happy. Presently we set forth; it was understood that we were going to his other house. On the walk, I found myself left behind and alone; the fears returned. Not far away there were lions, white ones, beneath a clump of trees; my fears vanished, of the lions and of being alone, and I recognised the animals as the beasts from *The Magic Flute*, gravely nodding their heads in time to the divine spell. I never got to the other house, but it did not matter, and presently we were all back where we had started, where more and more guests were arriving, and all were welcome. We began to drift back to the water's edge; we reboarded the boat. I knew nobody around me, and talked to none, but that did not matter either. Amid more laughter, the boat set off.

I awoke bathed in tears of joy, knowing where I had been, what door had been flung wide for me.

Bernard Levin
(from 'Enthusiasms')

Comfort

(Wilbur the pig has been watching the babies of his dead friend Charlotte the spider grow and begin to spin tiny webs.)

Then came a quiet morning when Mr Zuckerman opened a door on the north side. A warm draught of rising air blew softly through the barn cellar. The air smelt of the damp earth, of the spruce woods, of the sweet springtime. The baby spiders felt the warm updraught. One spider climbed to the top of the fence. Then it did something that came as a great surprise to Wilbur. The spider stood on its head, pointed its spinnerets in the air, and let loose a cloud of fine silk. The silk formed a balloon. As Wilbur watched, the spider let go of the fence and rose into the air.

'Goodbye!' it said, as it sailed through the doorway.

'Wait a minute!' screamed Wilbur. 'Where do you think you're going?'

But the spider was already out of sight...

Wilbur was frantic. Charlotte's babies were disappearing at a great rate.

'Come back, children!' he cried.

'Good-bye!' they called. 'Good-bye, good-bye!'

At last one little spider took time enough to stop and talk to Wilbur before making its balloon.

'We're leaving on the warm updraught. This is our moment for setting forth. We are aeronauts and we are going out into the world to make webs for ourselves.'

'But *where*?' asked Wilbur.

'Wherever the wind takes us. High, low. Near, far. East, west. North, south. We take to the breeze, we go as we please.'

'Are *all* of you going?' asked Wilbur. 'You can't *all* go. I would be left alone, with no friends. Your mother wouldn't want that to happen, I'm sure.'

The air was now so full of balloonists that the barn cellar looked almost as though a mist had gathered... He couldn't bear to watch any more. In sorrow he sank to the ground and closed his eyes. This seemed like the end of the world, to be deserted by Charlotte's children. Wilbur cried himself to sleep.

When he woke it was late afternoon. He looked at the egg sac. It was empty. He looked into the air. The balloonists were gone. Then he walked drearily to the doorway, where Charlotte's web used to be. He was standing there, thinking of her, when he heard a small voice.

'Salutations!' it said. 'I'm up here.'

'So am I,' said another tiny voice.

'So am I,' said a third voice. 'Three of us are staying. We like this place, and we like *you*.'

Wilbur looked up. At the top of the doorway three small webs were being constructed. On each web, working busily, was one of Charlotte's daughters.

'Can I take this to mean,' asked Wilbur, 'that you have definitely decided to live here in the barn cellar, and that I am going to have *three* friends?'

'You can indeed,' said the spiders.

'What are your names, please?' asked Wilbur, trembling with joy.

'I'll tell you my name,' replied the first little spider, 'if you'll tell me why you are trembling.'

'I'm trembling with joy,' said Wilbur.

'Then my name is Joy,' said the first spider.

E. B. White
(from 'Charlotte's Web')

Assurance

(Julian of Norwich was a nun who lived in the fifteenth century. She was a 'solitary', spending a life of prayer and meditation in a little 'cell' or room built on to a church. People visited her for help and counsel, and Julian shared with them her visions of God and her understanding of his love. 'Tempested', in the passage below, means 'tossed about by troubles as in a tempest'.)

Our Lord spoke these words with utter certainty:
'You will not be overcome.'

And these teachings and true comfort are for all my
fellow Christians...

The words 'You will not be overcome' were spoken
firmly
to give assurance and comfort
against all the troubles that might come.

He did not say, 'You will not be tempested,
you will not be troubled,
you will not be distressed.'

He said, 'You will not be overcome.'

Julian of Norwich

Faith

(During a hard winter in the Cumbrian fells, two boys, Harry and Bell, cycle to see a waterfall turned to icicles by the frost. Caught in a blizzard, they have to abandon their bikes and are rescued in the nick of time. Bell ends up in bed with bronchitis and Harry comes to see him.)

'I'm glad we went,' (said Harry). 'We saw the icicles.'

'You can't tell them about icicles. Icicles just got melted and gone. We never even got 'em home. I never showed 'em Grandad.'

'What's thou never showed Grandad?' said old Hewitson, lumping in.

'Icicles...'

'There seems a lot of things it's best to be quiet about,' said Harry. 'I suppose it's in case you don't get believed.'

'Oh *believed* is nothing,' said old Hewitson, producing chocolate cornflakes from somewhere. 'Getting believed's the least part of it. It's going about and seeing after things as matters. I's seed them icicles once, you's seed them once. Our Bell's seed them twice. I reckon we're all lucky. It's all that matters – seeing them. In fact maybe if you hadn't set out to see 'em, they wouldn't have been there. We'll never know.'

'What's that mean when it's at home?' said Bell.

'Tea's ready,' came a shout from downstairs.

'It means as it means. Think of sounds. Does it ever occur to thee, Bell Teesdale, Harry Bateman, that none of the sounds floating about the world wouldn't stand chance, stand *chance*, without ears ready for 'em?... Sounds need sounding boards of ears. Just think, before there was ears to reverberate off, there was not a sound in t'world – not even from oceans (not as I think a great deal of oceans, twice at Morecambe being very much a disappointment to me). And why not? Because sounds go floating about silent until there's an ear for 'em to come up against. Same thing with eyes for all I know. Icicles may need eyes to look at them.'

'There's no icicles for eyes to see now,' said Harry, watching the big splashing raindrops that had started to turn the yard below Bell's bedroom window to a sloppy black and white pudding. 'They're all gone.'

'Who's to say they're gone? Think it out. Just think it out. And Harry, come to thy tea. Bell's to look at the playing cards and have a sleep again – but he'll be up for Christmas and you'll be both away on them poor old bikes again.'

'Maybe there won't be any bikes. If any eyes fell on them. I'd not be surprised if they weren't there when we go looking for them – and nothing to do with magic.'

'Eyes did fall on 'em. A gypsy feller come round with them yesterday wanting reward, which your father gave him and a dozen eggs for luck. He'd had a hard walk through.'

'However did he know they were ours?' said Harry.

'I thowt gypsies were nowt but thieves,' said Bell.

'He knew,' said old Hewitson, 'he knew, and thief or no thief, he fetched 'em back. There's ways and means, and some folks' minds catches on in different ways than others. And there's many a thing you can't explain.'

Jane Gardam
(from 'The Hollow Land')

Without End

(After a spring wedding in a country church)

We went inside the church and the air still seethed quietly
with the wedding that was just over, it was warm with all
the breaths of the people and sweet with flowers and scent.
We stood very still by the altar, looking at a great vase of
white and yellow narcissi and apple blossom and I felt the
imprint of this marriage service somehow sinking gently
down and down on to us and being imprinted on to the
fabric of the church itself, into the stone of the walls and the
brass of the rails and the stained glass of the windows, being
absorbed, every hymn and anthem and voluntary, every
blessing and vow, every petitionary prayer, every praise in
the morning and thanksgiving at evening, every bidding of
welcome to a child and of farewell to a dead soul.

The church was empty apart from my daughter and me,
and it was not empty at all. She felt it, too. She wandered
quietly about, touching this and that, talking a little to
herself.

We closed the great door carefully, let down the latch, in
case a bird would get in and be trapped.

Outside, there were white and pink paper petals on the
ground, and spring sunshine.

Susan Hill
(from 'The Magic Apple Tree')

Without End

James ... turned away to go home by the short cut through the churchyard and over the wall into Pound Lane. It was, he thought, the most perfectly splendid evening he could remember. The sky was huge and clean and empty over Ledsham, a soft violet colour, with a feathery moon rising beyond the line of trees that fringed the churchyard. The trees were almost bare of leaves, their delicate branches splayed against the sky, loaded with the shaggy forms of rooks' nests. Above them, the rooks swirled and planed, rising and falling in invisible currents of air.

James walked down the path and then under the trees. Grey, ribbed trunks reached up and up over his head to meet a canopy of branches that was like the vaulting of a cathedral, and from this roof came spinning down dozens and hundreds of leaves. He looked at the branches near his head and saw suddenly that the new leaves were already there, sharp, folded shapes, shiny brown tips of beech and chestnut and elm. He walked on ... and the old leaves fell silently around him and piled up under his feet and above them the branches held up the new ones, furled and secret, waiting for the spring. Time reached away behind and ahead ... forward to other people who would leave their names in this place, look with different eyes on the same streets, rooftops, trees. And somewhere in the middle there was James, walking home for tea, his head full of confused but agreeable thoughts, hungry and a little tired, but content.

Penelope Lively
(from 'The Ghost of Thomas Kempe')

Sources and Acknowledgements

The editor and publishers gratefully acknowledge permission to reproduce the following copyright material:

HOT CROSS BUNS Jenny Overton: *The Ship from Simnel Street,* reprinted by permission of Faber and Faber Ltd.

EASTER EGGS Alison Uttley: from *The Country Child,* reprinted by permission of Faber and Faber Ltd.

EASTER CAKES Jenny Overton: from *The Ship from Simnel Street,* reprinted by permission of Faber and Faber Ltd.

LIGHT AND DARKNESS Leon Garfield: from *The Apprentices* (Puffin).

TAKE, EAT Brother Kenneth CGA: from *Pray With...* (Church House Publishing)

TAKE, EAT Mother Teresa: from *Pray With...* (Church House Publishing)

ARREST Esther Hautzig: from *The Endless Steppe* (Penguin) reprinted by permission of Hamish Hamilton.

ARREST Nan Goodall: from *Donkey's Glory* (Mowbray).

DENIAL Caroline Glyn: from *In Him was Life* (Gollancz).

SUFFERING Mike Gwilliam from the play *A Man Dies,* © Ivy Music Ltd.

DEATH Doris Buchanan Smith: from *A Taste of Blackberries* (Puffin).

GIVING Frances Hodgson Burnett: from *A Little Princess,* also published as *Sara Crewe.*

GIVING Sydney Carter: from *In the Present Tense* (Stainer and Bell Ltd.)

FOLLOWING Brian Wren: from *Mainly Hymns* (John Paul the Preacher's Press) reprinted by permission of Oxford University Press.

RESCUE Russell Hoban: from *The Mouse and his Child* (Puffin).

RESCUE Fay Sampson: from *Pangur Ban, the White Cat* (Lion).

SACRIFICE Fay Sampson: from *Pangur Ban, the White Cat* (Lion).

REPENTANCE C. S. Lewis: from *The Voyage of the Dawn Treader* (Collins).

MORNING Philip Larkin: from *The North Ship,* reprinted by permission of Faber and Faber Ltd.

NEW LIFE E. B. White: from *Charlotte's Web,* (Puffin).

RESURRECTION William Dunbar (written around 1500).

RESURRECTION Fay Sampson: from *Pangur Ban, the White Cat* (Lion).

VICTORY Colin Wood: from *The Alabama Story* (Rex Collings), also published as *A Confusion of Time* (Thos. Nelson Inc., USA).

LIBERATION Norman C. Habel: from *Interrobang* (Lutterworth Press).

WORD John Bell and Graham Maule: from *Wild Goose Songs, Vol. 1,* (Wild Goose Publications), © The Iona Community.

EASTER Jim Forest: from *Finding God among the Russians* (Lamp), reprinted by permission of Marshall, Morgan and Scott Ltd.

ACCEPTANCE Bernard Levin: from *Enthusiasms* (Sceptre), first published by Jonathan Cape Ltd.

COMFORT E. B. White: from *Charlotte's Web* (Puffin).

FAITH Jane Gardam: from *The Hollow Land* (Puffin).

WITHOUT END Susan Hill: from *The Magic Apple Tree* (Penguin), first published by Hamish Hamilton Ltd.

WITHOUT END Penelope Lively: from *The Ghost of Thomas Kempe* (a Piccolo book by Pan), first published by William Heinemann Ltd.